Marriage...

From "I Do"
to Forever

Edited by
Angela Joshi

Blue Mountain Press™
Boulder, Colorado

We gratefully acknowledge the permission granted by the following authors, publishers, and authors' representatives to reprint poems or excerpts from their publications: Susan Polis Schutz for "Love is the source of life," "In order to have...," "In marriage...," and "Together in marriage you will...." Copyright © 1982, 1988, 1989 by Stephen Schutz and Susan Polis Schutz. All rights reserved. PrimaDonna Entertainment Corp. for "Marriage Means Being Sweethearts for Life," "On your anniversary...," and "Our love is the one thing..." by Donna Fargo. Copyright © 2010 by PrimaDonna Entertainment Corp. All rights reserved. Candy Paull for "Your wedding day...." Copyright © 2010 by Candy Paull. All rights reserved. New Harbinger Publications, Inc., for "There are few occasions..." from THE CONSCIOUS BRIDE by Sheryl Paul. Copyright © 2000 by Sheryl Paul. All rights reserved. Cindy Chupack and Home Box Office, Inc., for "His hello was the end of her endings..." from "The Chicken Dance" from SEX AND THE CITY by Candace Bushnell. Copyright © 1999 by Cindy Chupack. All rights reserved. Alfred A. Knopf, a division of Random House, Inc., for "Let there be spaces..." from THE PROPHET by Kahlil Gibran. Copyright 1923 by Kahlil Gibran and renewed © 1951 by Administrators C.T.A. of Kahlil Gibran Estate, and Mary G. Gibran. All rights reserved. Michelle Mariotti for "The World of Marriage...." Copyright © 2010 by Michelle Mariotti. All rights reserved. HarperCollins Publishers for "The minute I heard..." from RUMI: THE BOOK OF LOVE: POEMS OF ECSTASY AND LONGING, TRANSLATIONS & COMMENTARY by Coleman Barks et al. Copyright © 2003 by Coleman Barks. All rights reserved. And for "Play allows tenderness..." from THE COUPLE'S COMFORT BOOK by Jennifer Louden. Copyright © 1994 by Jennifer Louden. All rights reserved.

Acknowledgments are continued on the last page.

Library of Congress Control Number: 2010905597
ISBN: 978-1-59842-528-4

█ and Blue Mountain Press are registered in U.S. Patent and Trademark Office. Certain trademarks are used under license.

Printed in China.
First Printing: 2010

♻ This book is printed on recycled paper.

This book is printed on paper that has been specially produced to be acid free (neutral pH) and contains no groundwood or unbleached pulp. It conforms with the requirements of the American National Standards Institute, Inc., so as to ensure that this book will last and be enjoyed by future generations.

Blue Mountain Arts, Inc.
P.O. Box 4549, Boulder, Colorado 80306

Contents

(Authors listed in order of first appearance)

Marriage Means Being Sweethearts for Life

Marriage is the gift that keeps on giving and the present that keeps on pleasing. It's the love that connects you to your favorite person in the world.

Marriage is a mutual trust and a vow you renew daily. It's putting each other first in the little things that matter a lot and the big things that help two people grow together. It's the promise you keep living up to, and it lasts forever and ever.

A happy marriage does more than stand the test of time. It causes two lives to sail toward eternity in each other's arms, learning lessons they couldn't learn alone or with anyone else. It's the source of joy that gives every day its smile. It's two sweethearts for life sharing dreams and trying to make them come true. Marriage is a celebration of eager promises and an endless number of beautiful tomorrows and happy anniversaries ever after.

— Donna Fargo

A Wedding Joins
Two Hearts

Your wedding day is a day
of dreams and destiny.
It's the beginning of
a new life together,
a love shared by two.
Begin with the intention
to cherish each other through
all the changes life brings,
stand with each other
and stand up for each other,
and commit to growing together
as a couple and as individuals.

Your wedding day is the first day
of the rest of your lives together.
It is a happy ending that
marks the beginning
of never-ending happiness.

* Candy Paull

There are few occasions in life more beautiful and awe-inspiring than a wedding. When two people decide to solidify their commitment, they begin the sacred journey of marriage, which begins with the engagement and continues through the rest of their lives.

※ Sheryl Paul

His hello was the end of her endings
Her laugh was their first step down the aisle
His hand would be hers to hold forever
His forever was as simple as her smile
He said she was what was missing
She said instantly she knew
She was a question to be answered
And his answer was "I do"

※ Cindy Chupack

Cherish each other
in big ways and in small ways,
and never forget the magic
of those three little words: "I love you."
In marriage, remember that
it is the little things that make the difference...
Don't forget the birthdays and the anniversaries.
An occasional note means a lot.
Share each other's life — even the small details —
for too often we forget that day-after-day becomes
year-after-year, and then it's gone.
Give each other room to grow...
We all need our time alone.
Keep strong your faith in each other;
time has a funny way of testing us,
and it's faith that gets us through.
Respect one another...
This world could always use more of that.
Speak your mind honestly, openly, but with kindness,
for angry words are scars that may never heal.
Trust each other; let your trust be your rock.
Most of all, each day...
be sure to hold each other
and fall in love all over again.

＊ Julia Escobar

Let there be spaces in your togetherness,
And let the winds of heaven dance between you.

Love one another, but make not a bond of love:
Let it rather be a moving sea between the shores
    of your souls.
Fill each other's cup but drink not from one cup.
Give one another of your bread but eat not from
    the same loaf.
Sing and dance together and be joyous, but let
    each one of you be alone,
Even as the strings of a lute are alone though they
    quiver with the same music.

Give your hearts, but not into each other's keeping.
For only the hand of Life can contain your hearts.
And stand together yet not too near together:
For the pillars of the temple stand apart,
And the oak tree and the cypress grow not in each
    other's shadow.

✳ Kahlil Gibran

The World of Marriage...

After the rice is thrown and the tuxedos are returned. After the thank-you cards are sent and the florist is paid in full. After the sunburn from your honeymoon starts to heal and the great photo of the wedding party slips into a frame. Then it can begin.

When the quiet settles around the two of you and it's no longer about fine-tuning the details of the event. When the phone rings less often and the mail begins to slow. When saying the words "husband" and "wife" no longer seems strange off the tongue.

When it starts to be about watching old movies together at two o'clock in the morning and grabbing him to slow dance while he shaves. When it's no longer about picking out china patterns, but rather about picking out food to put on them. When it's taking the car in for an oil change or fixing a favorite meal simply because it's Tuesday.

When you argue over money and make up over ice-cream cones in the park. When you hear his key click in the front door and it brings a smile to your lips. When you cuddle at night before the dreams come. When the world looks at the two of you but only sees a couple. Then, in those moments, hand in hand, the two of you leave the wedding behind and enter the world of marriage.

Michelle Mariotti

A Love Destined to Be

I love you as you are.
I love you as you will be.
I love you because there's this
little part of me (my heart)
that tells me that you and I
were simply and always
meant to be.
* Ashley Rice

The minute I heard my first love story
I started looking for you, not knowing
how blind that was.

Lovers don't finally meet somewhere.
They're in each other all along.

* Rumi

Yes, yours, my love, is the right human face.
I in my mind had waited for this long,
Seeing the false and searching for the true,
Then found you as a traveller finds a place
Of welcome suddenly amid the wrong
Valleys and rocks and twisting roads. But you,
What shall I call you? A fountain in a waste,
A well of water in a country dry,
Or anything that's honest and good, an eye
That makes the whole world bright.

* Edwin Muir

Two Lives Entwined

You and I
Have so much love,
That it
Burns like a fire,
In which we bake a lump of clay
Molded into a figure of you
And a figure of me.
Then we take both of them,
And break them into pieces,
And mix the pieces with water,
And mold again a figure of you,
And a figure of me.
I am in your clay.
You are in my clay.
In life we share a single quilt.
In death we will share one coffin.

Kuan Tao-shêng

I do not love you as if you were salt-rose,
   or topaz,
or the arrow of carnations the fire shoots off.
I love you as certain dark things are to be loved,
in secret, between the shadow and the soul.

I love you as the plant that never blooms
but carries in itself the light of hidden flowers;
thanks to your love a certain solid fragrance,
risen from the earth, lives darkly in my body.

I love you without knowing how, or when,
   or from where.
I love you straightforwardly, without complexities
   or pride;
so I love you because I know no other way

than this: where *I* does not exist, nor *you*,
so close that your hand on my chest is my hand,
so close that your eyes close as I fall asleep.

Pablo Neruda

Secrets to a Happy Marriage

Creating a storehouse of goodwill in the relationship is like putting money in the bank. These deposits can take many forms — a conversation, an episode of working out differences, a lingering gaze, or a sincere expression of gratitude — but they all have the common end of reaffirming our love and commitment, and they accumulate into a big tally. When there is an abundant account, you can make withdrawals when times are hard, and you live life with peace of mind, relishing a growing emotional wealth.

❋ Linda and Charlie Bloom

You promised to love and honor — the vows didn't say anything about becoming total bores. Being a couple doesn't mean cocooning with Moo Shoo for the rest of your lives. Corny as it sounds, you also need to get out there and keep your lives connected. The perfect couple's social life takes a balance of time together and time with friends (both sets).

❋ Carley Roney

When I meet a couple today that's been married for a long time, I ask them how they do it.... No matter who they are, they have something to teach me. One thing I hear over and over from couples who've made it work is that you must have respect for your partner, and you must be able to practice the art of forgiveness.

※ Maria Shriver

One of the best pieces of advice I've ever heard is that if you share your marital gripes with your friends or families, you will have their judgments and suggestions to contend with as well. And those may be more than a relationship can withstand. The person with whom you should talk about your feelings is your mate.

※ Joan Lunden

I'll tell you one secret to keeping the spark there: I think you've got to get away, just the two of you, with no kids. And you've got to spend time alone; you need to cultivate your own sense of self and nurture that as well.

※ Annette Bening

*H*appiness in marriage is not something that just happens. A good marriage must be created. In the art of marriage the *little things* are the *big things...*

It is never being too old to hold hands.

It is remembering to say, "I love you," at least once each day.

It is never going to sleep angry.

It is at no time taking the other for granted. The courtship shouldn't end with the honeymoon; it should continue through all the years.

It is having a mutual sense of values and common objectives; it is standing together facing the world.

It is forming a circle of love that gathers in the whole family.

It is doing things for each other, not in the attitude of duty or sacrifice, but in the spirit of joy.

It is speaking words of appreciation and demonstrating gratitude in thoughtful ways.

It is not expecting the husband to wear a halo
  or the wife to have the wings of an angel.
  It is not looking for perfection in each
  other. It is cultivating flexibility, patience,
  understanding and a sense of humor.
It is having the capacity to forgive and forget.
It is giving each other an atmosphere in which
  each can grow.
It is finding room for the things of the spirit.
  It is a common search for the good and
  the beautiful.
It is not only marrying the right partner; it is
  being the right partner.

✳ Wilferd A. Peterson

I used to think that being in love
Meant passion, excitement, and romance.
Now I understand that real love
    is all those things,
But it's so much more...

Love is...
Watching television together,
Sharing Sunday-morning newspapers,
Talking through our problems,
Reading next to each other in bed,
Cuddling when the nights get cold,
And knowing we will always be together.

Being with you has shown me
All that love can be.
I'm so glad I get to share my life
And my love with you.

✳ Jason Blume

True love is being the best of friends —
being able to say and share anything while
still being sensitive to the other's feelings...
It's when you always think of the future
in terms of "we" instead of "me."

※ Tim Tweedie

You are truly the love of my life,
the person my soul searched endlessly for
and now has found its other half.

You are the person who knows me best,
the one I can share everything with,
the one who loves me for who I am
and makes me a better person.

You will always be my lover,
my soul mate, and the person
I consider to be my very best friend.

※ Elle Mastro

Love is the miracle that can take two lives and mold them into one, take two souls and bind them for life.

＊ Michele Weber

There is only one happiness in life, to love and be loved.

＊ George Sand

Love doesn't make the world go round. Love is what makes the ride worthwhile.

＊ Franklin P. Jones

Nothing is sweeter than love,
Nothing stronger,
Nothing higher,
Nothing wider,
Nothing more pleasant,
Nothing fuller or better
in heaven or earth.

※ Thomas à Kempis

Love is the source of life.

※ Susan Polis Schutz

Tips for Her

The best thing that no one tells the bride is that there is no one method for marriage, at least not for happy ones. First, you plan a wedding that befits you. And then, by trial and error, you learn what works for you in *your* marriage, in your household, in the juggling of careers and finances....

In essence, you sculpt your own union, a marriage as devoted and as traditional in some respects as good marriages always are, but in other ways as zany and liberating as your experience of life when you were single. You throw out as much of the institution as you want to, or as much as you can, and you make your own marriage.

※ Marg Stark

In order to have a successful marriage
you must put out of your mind
any lessons learned from previous relationships
because if you carry a sensitivity or fear with you
you won't be acting freely
and you won't let yourself be really known

※ Susan Polis Schutz

*F*irst thing you do is tell your husband he is perfect in every way. Here's why this works so well. All men feel deep down inside that they are, in fact, *perfect in every way*. It's their mothers' fault. If you happen to mention that you also find this true, they will think you're a genius and will be much more likely to do almost any dang thing you tell them.

※ Patricia Heaton

I'm going to share with you something that may seem plain silly, but that will help you better know and love your man: It's quite possible that your husband is one of many men who need to feel like a hero.

The bottom line: Your husband may think he's Superman and you're Lois Lane. He's Spiderman; you're Mary Jane. You get the idea. You can laugh about it if you want, or you can outright ignore it, but if you treat your husband like someone who has helped save your life, he'll be motivated day in and day out to swoop in and do it over and over again.

※ Scott Haltzman, MD

Tips for Him

Responsible men know that they need to get their car serviced. You change the oil every 5,000 miles, put gas in, and get the brakes checked. Romance is the equivalent of relationship maintenance. Take your wife out for a date, bring her a gift for no reason, praise her regularly, and touch her lovingly. Regular romance is better than any single gesture of love over time.

❋ Cory Huff

Think like part of a team. If there is a problem, assume your wife is on your side and wants to work with you to figure out a solution. Your wife is not the enemy. You can work together to problem-solve creatively, and to have more of your legitimate needs met. Nothing warms a woman's heart like hearing the word "we." Use it often.

❋ Cait Johnson

We men may say to ourselves, "I went out and did all the things you told me to today. I made your coffee. I put away the groceries. Doesn't that say that I love you?"

Well, no. It doesn't. Because, fellow men, when it comes to communicating love to your wife, you have to actually state it aloud.

※ Scott Haltzman, MD

Like all relationships, marriage requires great heaps of understanding in the most basic ways.

When Mary and I were first married she would leave her shoes by whatever door she used to walk into the house. Mary has lots of shoes, so there would be five or six pairs scattered around. I'm a neat freak. After six months I said, "Love [as we've always called each other], why don't you just put these little piles of shoes in the closet?" Without missing a beat she said, "If these little piles of shoes weren't here, you'd miss them." Meaning, if she weren't here, I'd miss her. You know what? I found I could live with a few shoes here and there.

※ Sam Haskell

Marriage and Commitment

Making a commitment on your wedding day takes one little "I do." Living the commitment every day takes a lot of doing....

My point is that marriage isn't just a state of being. It requires time, thought, and attention. It's a million separate actions taken in order to stay with someone, share a life with someone, have a partnership with someone, appreciate and support someone, cultivate love with someone — actions taken consistently over the long haul.

✳ Maria Shriver

The adage "give and you will receive" was probably first pronounced by a happily married couple who learned over the years that if you give to someone genuine happiness by catering to that person's needs (even when you don't always agree or fully understand), you are far more likely to receive kindness and happiness in return.

✳ Scott Haltzman, MD

What makes some relationships last a lifetime? It's a commitment to work together through all of life's ups and downs... and there will be ups and downs. You're not necessarily going to feel "full of love" for your mate all the time. That doesn't have to mean the relationship is in real trouble — commitment is about sticking around and trusting that those feelings will come back.

✳ Joan Lunden

The truth is, I thank God every day for inventing marriage. The way I see it, I'm lucky to have found a woman who will put up with me, and marriage makes it so she can't leave without a hassle.

I do make jokes about it, but I enjoy all the benefits of marriage.

✳ Ray Romano

The Importance of Romance

In order for love to thrive, not just survive,
it needs a protective environment.
We call it romance,
and it is as necessary to love
as the air we breathe is to living.
Love can't exist in a vacuum.
It needs more than two individuals
staring blankly at each other.
For love to grow, the two people need to
    communicate.
The sounds, smells, sights, and touches
that are the main ingredients of love
must somehow be passed back and forth
between the lovers.
Romance is the medium
for this transferal.

— Dr. Ruth K. Westheimer

Romance... is simply a way of thinking and behaving that lets someone special know they are a top priority in your life... It's wanting to spend time with someone, making new memories, creating excitement, having fun, and sharing adventures. It's putting in that extra effort to ensure that someone knows how you feel. It's knowing that great relationships require nurturing and attention to thrive.

※ Gwendolyn Gray

The words *husband* and *wife* should not be synonymous with *roommate*. Love should not be mundane. It should not be banal. When it becomes that, it loses its magic. While the comforts of shared coffee cups, someone to sort through the bills with, conversations about the children, and admissions of fear to one who has become your best friend are all a part of what make long-term nesting wonderful, emotionally it is to our peril when we allow considerations of the world to form a veil across the face of love....

Romantic love is a force of nature. Like an ancient goddess, it likes to receive gifts. It must be honored, respected, protected, and cherished.

※ Marianne Williamson

Fighting and Making Up

It's normal to fight. I look forward to that point, and I hear about people that have been married a long time, that they start to fight and then they start laughing at each other. That's the ultimate point.

※ Jerry Seinfeld

Maybe we don't always see eye to eye, but that doesn't make us unusual; it makes us individuals. We are two people with separate points of view, ideas, and ways of doing things. But these differences help us to enhance our relationship and celebrate what is unique in each of us.

It doesn't mean that we're incompatible — just a little stubborn. But I enjoy sharing my life with someone who challenges my thoughts and isn't afraid to have an opinion different from mine.

※ T. L. Nash

[My wife] can find the humor in everything. This is the key to the success of our marriage. But I won't lie and tell you we don't have bumps in the road. Humor always seems to rescue us from the precipice.

There is one particular example when Terry told me: "That's it, I'm out!" She ran to the door, turned to me very dramatically, and declared, "**I will send for my things!**"

I waited a beat and then asked, "What did you just say?"

She repeated, "I will send for my things."

First of all, I had never heard that statement outside of a movie. So I asked, "Who will you send and what specific things will you be sending them for?"

After a long, dramatic, painstaking pause, a smile appeared on Terry's face. And then slowly she began to laugh. So did I. There are very few women who would find the humor in this otherwise serious situation. As we both laughed together at the absurdity of her statement, we embraced. The fight was over.

✳ Howie Mandel

Laughter and Fun

If you can't remember the last time you and
your partner had some fun together — just
plain old fun — then you are long overdue....

It doesn't matter if you're out at the movies
together or barefoot in the park. It doesn't
matter if you're playing soccer or Twister. It
doesn't matter if you're laughing out loud or
just smiling and feeling happy. All that matters
is your willingness to take time as a couple
for play. It's an indispensable ingredient in
the day-to-day recipe that yields the delicious
feeling of being liked.

✳ Steven Carter

I married my wife because she makes me
laugh. You should never marry someone who
doesn't make you laugh.

✳ Garrison Keillor

Laughter is one of the best things you can share with your spouse. It releases stress, amplifies joy, increases intimacy, and helps create some of the happiest memories you'll share in life together. So make sure you get some good, quality laughter in every day, because it's true: those who laugh together, stay together.

＊ Sara Emerson

Play allows tenderness and animosity to exist side by side, and frolics relieve the tedium of life. Which sounds like more fun: screaming uncontrollably because your partner is eating with his or her mouth open *yet again* or putting on a plastic pig nose and continuing to eat your dinner?

＊ Jennifer Louden

Support and Strength

To love someone deeply
Gives you strength.

Being loved by someone deeply
Gives you courage.

　　　　　　　* Lao-Tzu

When two people are at one
　　in their inmost hearts,
They shatter even the strength of
　　iron or bronze.
And when two people
　　understand each other
　　in their inmost hearts,
Their words are sweet and strong,
　　like the fragrance of orchids.

　　　　　　　　* I Ching

*H*usbands and wives are designed to complement each other. When the man is weak, his wife is strong; when she stumbles, he is there to pick her up. Life is easier when two hearts and minds are committed to working together to face the challenges of the day.

※ Gary D. Chapman

*W*hen all appears lost, I look to Tracy to help me find it again — or, better yet, be with me for as long as it takes for something new to arrive. And longer.

※ Michael J. Fox

15 Things That Are Great About Marriage

* Every blessing is doubled

* Every trouble is divided

* It's the ultimate expression of love between two people

* It's a gift you get to open every day of your lives

* It understands and forgives... always

* It encourages and nurtures new life and new experiences

* You trust each other completely

* You get to share the kind of happiness only the most fortunate ever find

* It deepens and enriches every facet of life

* A million little things every day remind you why you fell in love

* Any day of the week can be "date night"

* Household chores go twice as fast when you work as a team

* You always have someone to split dessert with

* You can always make each other laugh

* The longer you're together, the happier you are

For My Wife

Sometimes it might seem like I take for granted all the things you do. Even though I may not say the words as often as I should, I hope you know how grateful I am for you.

Every day, I realize more and more how lucky I am to have you. Even when our days get hectic and the world's demands take over, my heart is always saying a silent "thank you" for the gift of your love.

Thank you for all the things you do. You are the best part of my life. You bring me more happiness than I've ever known. You are everything to me... the love of my life... my wonderful, beautiful wife.

✳ R. Taylor

To My Husband

We share a bond too deep for words and a friendship I celebrate every day of the year. It feels so good to know you're always there for me — listening to my dreams and being interested in my world.

The moments we spend together talking, laughing, and listening have made the years so special and have given me a treasured gift of memories I cherish. We've been through everything together — pulling for each other and revealing strengths we didn't even know we had.

What really makes our marriage special is you — your sacrifice and support, understanding and faithfulness, strength and love. Though the years will bring changes, you will always be perfect in my eyes. Though life may bring challenges, you'll always be first in my heart. You're the sunshine in my life, the hero in my world, and I love you very much.

✳ Linda E. Knight

Being Married to You
Is like Sharing Every Day
with My Best Friend

I can't imagine life without you.
My heart aches just at the thought.
With you, I have laughed until I cried at
private jokes no one else would understand.
I have cried until I ached
when life's realities crashed into my world
and I sought comfort in your waiting arms.
It is impossible for me to explain
    to anyone else
how much you mean to me.
They just wouldn't understand.
You and I exist as two individuals
but function as one.

I can share all my thoughts
and feelings with you,
and I know that you will listen
      and not judge.
You are the one person I need
to share everything with
without hesitation and
without regret.
I think it is rare to have
      such a friendship in marriage,
and every day I want to tell you
exactly how much that means to me —
how I'd be lost without you,
silenced without your touch.
But when our eyes meet
and you smile,
I somehow know
that I need not say a word
for you to truly understand.

※ Susan Farrell

Sharing the Years Together

Grow old along with me,
the best is yet to be.

✳ Robert Browning

We used to count the months,
loving hearts circled on the calendar.
Now we count the years,
measuring the elusive time
that has seeped through the lovely hourglass
    of our marriage —
minutes, hours, days, years, accumulating
    like jewels,
blurring into blue-gray memory.

Time, it occurs to me, is such a funny way
    to calculate
the playful glances between spoonfuls of soup
and the endless card games — meaningless,
yet we sit together for hours...

Do you remember my wedding dress,
    crisp white and beaded,
and the beads that fell off
by the end of the night —
little gems lost forever, like the minutes escaping
    into the chasms of time
that we chase after and count,
    one day a year,
to remember the sparkle of my tiara,
your clean-shaven young face.

And tomorrow, when the count starts again,
when the heavy hourglass is turned over,
I will heat up leftovers for dinner and
you will wash the dishes, I hope.
Perhaps we will play Scrabble,
and I will cheat. And the days
will continue as such.
I giggle
with food stuck in my teeth,
and you laugh at me with
love in your eyes. And we
ignore the clock, ticking on the wall,
trying to force us to leave the moment.

※ Chaya Steinman

The nicest feeling I've ever known is being in love with you. And I want to thank you for these feelings...

For bringing me happiness as though it were a gift I could open every day... I am grateful to you. For letting me share the most personal parts of your world... I am indebted to you. For being everything that you are to me, and for doing it so beautifully... I thank you with all my heart.

＊ D. Pagels

I'm planning on being madly in love with you for the rest of my life. And if it's all right with you, I'm going to be thanking you forever... for making me a hundred times happier than I ever imagined I could be.

＊ Lorrie Westfall

My spouse, my lover, my friend. Do you know how often I give thanks for you each day? When I watch you sleeping, I give thanks for comfort. When I see you caring for our home, I give thanks for safety. For the person you are, I give thanks. For the trust that lives between us, I give thanks. For your painstaking attention to the details that matter most, for all that we know and all that we have yet to learn together, for sadness, for joy, I give thanks.

✳ Rachel Snyder

Anniversaries Are Beautiful Reminders

Anniversaries are times to reflect on and remember, times to celebrate and embrace the blessings that come from being together ✳ They are sweet, joyful confirmations ✳ They are milestones in life, looking back on a memory-filled past ✳ They are touchstones for the future, linking together plans and dreams ✳ When two people share so much, their days, their hopes, and their journey, there is little that compares with the smiles that can shine in the hearts of a husband and a wife ✳

Anniversaries are blessings the passing years bring ✳ And they are beautiful reminders that nothing is better than being with the one you love... all the days of your life ✳

✳ Casey Whilson

On your anniversary, take the time to remember back to when you first met. Reflect on the joy you've known since then, the ways you've grown, and the fact that you're changing still.

Remember the promises you made to each other, and renew your commitment to be there with each other always. Soak in the blessings of your togetherness, and look around you and compare the prize you found in each other and the life you've shared since day one. Bask in the good fortune of your relationship. Look forward to tomorrow together, forever joined as one.

＊ Donna Fargo

I Want to Say More Than Just "I Love You"

Sometimes it's not enough just to say
   "I love you."
Even though I do love you,
I feel I need to express more,
because there is so much more to
   our relationship.
Sometimes I need to tell you
you're the love I live for,
you're my dream made into reality.
Yours are the arms that
hold me close,
and it is your smile that brings
a ray of sunshine
to even the darkest of days.

You are the one who tells me
to keep believing in myself,
in you, and in us.
You have become a part of me
I could never live without,
and as long as I'm living,
as long as you care,
I'll be here for you.
I'll do anything for you.
I love you.

＊ Janine Stahl

Marriage Is Forever

In marriage
two people share
all their dreams and goals
their weaknesses and strengths
In marriage
two people share
all the joys and sadnesses of life
and all the supreme pleasures
In marriage
two people share
all of their emotions and feelings
all of their tears and laughter

Marriage is the most
fulfilling relationship
one can have
and the love that you share
as husband and wife
is beautifully forever

✳ Susan Polis Schutz

A deal is a deal. To me, that just says it all. Marriage is for keeps.

※ Courteney Cox Arquette

Our love is the one thing I trust to last forever. I believe it will stand the test of time and circumstance. It inspires my confidence and devotion. It guides me, empowers me, and motivates me to hope and dream.

I love you unconditionally, always. You are my life, and your love is the greatest gift I've ever known.

※ Donna Fargo

Together in marriage
you will bring out the best
in each other
You will learn from each other
and grow from your differences
You will be two individuals
living your own lives
with each other as one

Together in marriage
you will be stronger
more sensitive
more aware, more knowing
and more at peace
than you are individually
You will be better people

Together in marriage
your love will give understanding
to all that you do
because you will share
your ideas, goals
and frustrations
And you will always have
someone to support
whatever you say and do

Together in marriage
you will be able
to achieve
all that you want
in life

※ Susan Polis Schutz

Acknowledgments continued...

We gratefully acknowledge the permission granted by the following authors, publishers, and authors' representatives to reprint poems or excerpts from their publications: Faber & Faber Limited for "Yes, yours, my love..." from "The Confirmation" from THE NARROW PLACE by Edwin Muir. Copyright © 1943 by Edwin Muir. All rights reserved. New Directions Publishing Corp. for "You and I..." from "Married Love" by Kuan Tao-Shêng from WOMEN POETS OF CHINA, translated by Kenneth Rexroth and Ling Chung. Copyright © 1973 by Kenneth Rexroth and Ling Chung. All rights reserved. University of Texas Press for "I do not love you as if you were..." from 100 LOVE SONNETS: CIEN SONETOS DE AMOR by Pablo Neruda, translated by Stephen Tapscott. Copyright © Pablo Neruda 1959 and Fundacion Pablo Neruda. Copyright © 1986 by the University of Texas Press. Reprinted by permission. All rights reserved. New World Library, Novato, CA, www.newworldlibrary.com, for "Creating a storehouse of goodwill..." from 101 THINGS I WISH I KNEW WHEN I GOT MARRIED by Charlie and Linda Bloom. Copyright © 2004 by Charlie and Linda Bloom. All rights reserved. Crown Publishing Group, a division of Random House, Inc., for "You promised to love and honor..." from THE NEST NEWLYWED HANDBOOK by Carley Roney. Copyright © 2006 by The Knot, Inc. All rights reserved. Grand Central Publishing for "When I meet a couple today..." and "Making a commitment..." from TEN THINGS I WISH I'D KNOWN BEFORE I WENT OUT INTO THE REAL WORLD by Maria Shriver. Copyright © 2000 by Maria Shriver. Reprinted by permission of Grand Central Publishing. All rights reserved. Joan Lunden Productions, www.joanlunden.com, for "One of the best pieces of advice..." and "What makes some relationships..." from WAKE-UP CALLS: MAKING THE MOST OF EVERY DAY by Joan Lunden. Copyright © 2001 by New Life Entertainment, Inc. All rights reserved. Liz Smith for "I'll tell you one secret..." by Annette Bening from "Annette Bening: at lunch with Liz" (*Good Housekeeping*: November 2004). Copyright © 2004 by Liz Smith. All rights reserved. Heacock Literary Agency, Inc., for "Happiness in marriage is..." from THE ART OF LIVING by Wilferd A. Peterson. Copyright © 1960, 1961 by Wilferd A. Peterson. All rights reserved. Jason Blume for "I used to think that being in love...." Copyright © 2007 by Jason Blume. All rights reserved. Hyperion for "The best thing that no one tells..." from WHAT NO ONE TELLS THE BRIDE by Marg Stark. Copyright © 1998 by Marg Stark. Reprinted by permission. All rights reserved. And for "When all appears lost..." from ALWAYS LOOKING UP by Michael J. Fox. Copyright © 2009 by Michael J. Fox. Reprinted by permission. All rights reserved. Ballantine Books, a division of Random House, Inc., for "First thing you do is tell..." from MOTHERHOOD AND HOLLYWOOD: HOW TO GET A JOB LIKE MINE by Patricia Heaton. Copyright © 2003 by Patricia Heaton. All rights reserved. And for "Like all relationships..." from PROMISES I MADE MY MOTHER by Sam Haskell with David Rensin. Copyright © 2009 by Sam Haskell. All rights reserved. John Wiley and Sons, Inc., for "I'm going to share with you..." and "The adage..." from THE SECRETS OF HAPPILY MARRIED WOMEN by Scott Haltzman, MD and Theresa Foy DiGeronimo. Copyright © 2008 by Scott Haltzman. All rights reserved. And for "We men may say to ourselves..." from THE SECRETS OF HAPPILY MARRIED MEN by Scott Haltzman, MD with Theresa Foy DiGeronimo. Copyright © 2006 by Scott Haltzman. All rights reserved. Corey Huff for "Responsible men know that..." from "Romance? What Is Romance?" (agoodhusband.net: February 9, 2010). Copyright © 2010 by Cory Huff. All rights reserved. Cait Johnson for "Think like part of a team" from "Be a Good Husband: 5 More Guidelines" (care2.com: May 16, 2002). Copyright © 2002 by Cait Johnson. All rights reserved. Bantam Books, a division of Random House, Inc., for "The truth is..." from EVERYTHING AND A KITE by Ray Romano. Copyright © 1998 by Luckykids, Inc. All rights reserved. And for "[My wife] can find the humor..." from HERE'S THE DEAL: DON'T TOUCH ME by Howie Mandel. Copyright © 2009 by Alevy Productions, Inc. All rights reserved. Dr. Ruth K. Westheimer for "In order for love to thrive" from 52 LESSONS ON COMMUNICATING LOVE. Copyright © 2004 by Dr. Ruth K. Westheimer. All rights reserved. Hay House, Inc., Carlsbad, CA, for "The words *husband* and *wife*..." from THE AGE OF MIRACLES: EMBRACING THE NEW MIDLIFE by Marianne Williamson. Copyright © 2008 by Marianne Williamson. All rights reserved. T. L. Nash for "Maybe we don't always see...." Copyright © 2010 by T. L. Nash. All rights reserved. Fred Topol for "It's normal to fight" by Jerry Seinfeld from "Jerry Seinfeld: 'Emotion and Conflict Is the Essence of Comedy'" (Starpulse.com: February 25, 2010). Copyright © 2010 by Fred Topol. All rights reserved. M. Evans, an imprint of Taylor Trade Publishing, for "If you can't remember..." from THIS IS HOW LOVE WORKS by Steven Carter. Copyright © 2001 by Steven Carter. All rights reserved. Prairie Home Productions, LLC, for "I married my wife..." by Garrison Keillor from "Keillor Instinct" by Paul Engleman (*AARP Magazine*: March/April 2005). Copyright © 2005 by Garrison Keillor. All rights reserved. Tyndale House Publishers, Inc., for "Husbands and wives are designed..." from THE FOUR SEASONS OF MARRIAGE by Gary D. Chapman. Copyright © 2005 by Gary Chapman. All rights reserved. Chaya Steinman for "We used to count the months...." Copyright © 2010 by Chaya Steinman. All rights reserved. Rachel Snyder for "My spouse, my lover, my friend." Copyright © 2007 by Rachel Snyder. All rights reserved. Colleen Rush for "A deal is a deal..." by Courteney Cox Arquette from "Revealed! 101 Secrets to a Happy Marriage" (*Redbook*: April 2003). Copyright © 2003 by Colleen Rush. All rights reserved.

A careful effort has been made to trace the ownership of selections used in this anthology in order to obtain permission to reprint copyrighted material and give proper credit to the copyright owners. If any error or omission has occurred, it is completely inadvertent, and we would like to make corrections in future editions provided that written notification is made to the publisher:

BLUE MOUNTAIN ARTS, INC., P.O. Box 4549, Boulder, Colorado 80306